21ST CENTURY BUSINESS CARD

SPEAK VOLUMES ABOUT YOUR PROFESSIONAL CREDIBILITY —24 HOURS A DAY, 7 DAYS A WEEK!

NIKKI COOPER

21ST CENTURY BUSINESS CARD
Copyright © 2015 by Nikki Cooper.

Nikki runs Seminars, Workshops and Events teaching people how to manifest abundance and prosperity and develop a success mindset in business.

Contact Nikki:	nikki@nikkicooper.com
Skype:	lifestyleplus1
Phone:	0414 638 552
Website:	www.nikkicooper.com
	www.amazon.com/author/nikkicooper
	www.selfpublisherssummit.com

"A successful self-publisher must fill three roles: Author, Publisher, and Entrepreneur—or APE."

— Guy Kawasaki, APE: Author, Publisher, Entrepreneur. How to Publish a Book

"I have always believed that if you think it, dream it feel it, you WILL achieve it."

Nikki Cooper

"Go APE: Author a great book, Publish it quickly, and Entrepreneur your way to success. Self-publishing isn't easy, but it's fun and sometimes even lucrative. Plus, your book could change the world."

—Guy Kawasaki, APE: Author, Publisher, Entrepreneur. How to Publish a Book

"I'm tired of the anonymity of being an unpublished author. I crave the anonymity of being self-published."

—Tristan Durie, The Paperless Indetective

"Only a few short years ago, the average stay-at-home mum spent her relaxation time reading Jackie Collins and staring at the pool boy. Now, half of them are outselling Jackie Collins writing porn about the pool boy. The other half are writing reviews of them."

—Pete Morin

"You must be the change you wish to see in the world."

—Mahatma Gandhi

"You are not your resume, you are your work."

—Seth Godin

"One finds limits by pushing them."

—Herbert Simon

"You only have to do a very few things right in your life so long as you don't do too many things wrong."

—Warren Buffett

"Even if you are on the right track, you'll get run over if you just sit there."

—Will Rogers

TABLE OF CONTENTS

FOREWORD
1500 Weekends Left

Let me tell you a little secret before we begin. In 1998 on 2nd July, I attended a Seminar in Sydney Australia.

The name of the event was 'Born Rich' and it was conducted by a gentleman who empowered us with knowledge and tools to tap into our inherent greatness and fulfill our 'magnificent potential'.

At the conclusion of the Seminar, the Speaker said, 'Now go and apply all this information because most of you in this room have only 1500 weekends left!' His words rocked me to the core and every single weekend since 1998 I actually count the number of weekends I have left. It's only an estimate but you get the idea!

1500 weekends is not a huge amount of time to be the 'success story' you were born to be. Time moves too quickly. The days pass by and it seems as though we're spinning our wheels.

Yesterday's barriers remain in place. We might be doing okay, but we are still being dragged down by the same problems that held us back last year. No matter whom you are or what your lifework may be, you are playing checkers with time. Move with quick decision and time will favour you.

Stand still and time will wipe you off the board.

Nikki Cooper
June 2015

INTRODUCTION:
WELCOME TO THIS BOOK

"You are a start-up... The next great business is you."
—*Hugh Howey*

"You'll learn that the key to a great book is editing — grinding, buffing, and polishing — not writing."
—*Guy Kawasaki, APE: Author, Publisher, Entrepreneur. How to Publish a Book*

If you've been searching for a new way to reach your customers, or establish credibility for yourself as a job seeker or business owner, then you are in the right place at the right time.

Because I am about to hand YOU **the secret** to making more sales.

Because I am about to hand you the opportunity to blow the socks off an employer when you next apply for a job.

Because I am going to show you how to give a prospect a business card <u>they won't forget</u>.

Because you're about to discover a way to legally and ethically get off the so-called 'ladder of success' – skip the ladder altogether – and quickly be seen as the authority in your field.

Hi. My name is **Nikki Cooper** and I've been helping others achieve success since creating my first self-development program way back in 1977. Not 1997. *Nineteen Seventy Seven.* A lot of people calling themselves 'internet marketers' will tell you they started out in 1997. And for most of them it's true. By 1997, I was a 20 year veteran.

Fast forward to 2015 I am a public speaker and self-publishing guru and the founder of the Australian Self-Publishing Summit. My passion is helping people achieve their goals and dreams and I believe a little book is the way to do it. I should know, I have written 5 books in 2 years all through the amazing technology we have at our fingertips today. Now it's your turn.

I did well in high school – but when that finished, I suddenly had to think about a career –I had a passion for helping young people – so I became a high school teacher, starting out in a country town 900km from home. The remoteness, the culture shock, the oppressive heat made it a testing time for me – but in 1977 I was invited to work on a **Personal Development Program** for the students.

It didn't take long – I was hooked on helping people improve their lives and to this day I get a kick out of seeing people succeed. However things didn't exactly go to plan in my own life...

After a brief marriage and painful divorce, I found myself wandering into a bookstore one day and I'm not sure if it was just pure luck, or a subconscious attraction, but I stumbled into the self-help section and the answers appeared before me. The books there reminded me of my own personal development course I'd created back in '77 and I could see I wasn't following my own principles. Time for action!

From that day, I could feel my whole life shifting and gaining traction. I began to improve every area of my life and I have never looked back.

And it call came from BOOKS...books just like the one you're reading now!

"Authors today need a publisher as much as they need a tapeworm in their guts."

—Rayne Hall

Enough about *me*, this is about **YOU**.

As I mentioned before, I have a secret for you, a secret which, when you understand it, will make you wonder why you didn't think of it yourself. You'll wonder why more business owners don't do it. And best of all, you'll be excited at the thought of **making a real impact** with your prospects...

'There's no shortage of remarkable ideas, what's missing is the will to execute them"

—Seth Godin

THE ULTIMATE BUSINESS CARD

"Call it a business card, a resume, a billboard, or whatever you choose, but the short of it is that books are no longer just books. They are branding devices and credibility signals"
—*Ryan Holiday*
www.FastCompany.com

Picture it...you're at a networking event. Meeting people, shaking hands, doing the 'corporate handshake' that is, exchanging business cards. Or you have just applied for your first job and there a thousand other candidates on the market. In this uncertain economy how are you going to really stand out? When you arrive at the office for your interview, you hand your prospective employer your little book. When he or she sees you are an author, then you will stand a very good chance of achieving your goal of standing head and shoulders above the rest.

YOUR business card is different...

When people get your little book, a look of surprise comes over their face. They can't believe you just handed them such a valuable and generous gift and it takes them a few moments to actually realize that yes, this actually IS your business card.

Your business card doesn't get stuck in the glove box of the car. **Your business card** doesn't get thrown in a handbag side pocket and forgotten. **Your business card** doesn't get dropped in a bin on the way out of the building.

Nope. **YOUR** business card gets brought home and shown off to the rest of the family. Your business card gets <u>placed with care on a shelf</u>, either at home or the office, within arm's length of the desk where the business decisions are made. Your business card gets taken off the shelf, carefully examined and those all-important business decisions are made based on the advice YOUR business card provides.

Because your business card is a <u>book</u>.

Yes, just like the one you're reading now, your business card is a real life, black & white, paper-and-ink book. I'm here to make **YOU a published author** and highly sought-after business person in your field of expertise.

I know what you're thinking – I couldn't just give everyone I meet a book, can I? Surely, there are just so many reasons why this isn't feasible. I get you – this may be a new idea for you and even if you've heard it before, you may be under the impression it won't work for you. Like anything, there are plenty of myths surrounding this kind of marketing...

5 Book Publishing Myths Busted:

1. *It's too expensive* – In reality, I've got plenty of different ways to publish a book without breaking the bank in anyway – this is the age of information and there are so many companies providing dirt cheap book publishing services, you won't need to spend much money at all...but **the return on**

your investment will be <u>spectacular</u>... and you'll never waste your hard-earned money on normal business cards again.

Listen – you've got to know the **Lifetime Value Of A Customer,** or LVC. Let's say you are a personal injury lawyer, running a small practice, wondering how you can get ahead of all the other law firms in the city. Everyone knows how competitive law is these days. In my state of NSW there is an oversupply of lawyers. Calculate the average fee of a client for however long they use your services, for this example we'll just say its $5,000. For every person that comes in, sits on the other side of your desk and enquires about your legal services, 20% of them become your paying clients.

So, for every five people you get into your office, you make $5,000. Some pay more, some pay less, some stay longer, some don't, but you've averaged out all your clients and all payments to a figure of five grand. This is **your** LVC.

Now, you're going to write a book about the '**Top 3 Ways To Maximise Your Personal Injury Claim**', or something like that. You've got plenty of case studies and data to use and you're going to find out about some easy ways to get that material into a book without gluing yourself to the computer for hours and hours, after you should have gone home.

Imagine the reaction of your prospects when you hand the book over! At first they may think it's something for them to read, so you'll have to be clear when you say "this is for you." As you'll see throughout this book, your conversion rate is going to go through the roof when you start doing this! Your book will automatically give you absolute 'expert status' – and that's a given in your prospect's mind, when there are 7 other personal injury lawyers in this part of town and you're number 3 in a series of 7 free 1st appointments your potential client has booked.

You won't need to be shy about closing the person on hiring you, because not only are you now an **unquestioned expert**, but you've given them something for free and they weren't expecting that at all. Even if they somehow escape into the street and even if they persevere through the rest of their appointments, none of the other lawyers will extend such an unexpected gift. Not one. Who do you think is going to stick in your potential clients' minds? Who is going to get the call? **You**.

In this book you'll find examples of people doubling their closing rate doing just this. What does that mean in numbers for you? If you get 10 people in for a free 1st interview and you're currently closing 2 of them and making $10,000 on average, when you start handing out your book and doing absolutely nothing else different and you start closing 4 out of 10 instead of 2 now... that $10,000 has turned itself into $20,000. All from some paper, ink and smart thinking on your part.

In fact, if you convert just one extra client that's an extra $5,000 in fees – and **you** get to be known as the generous expert who gives out free books.

2. *I wouldn't know what to write about* – In this book I'm going to show you exactly how **you can have a book** with relevant content, **which your prospects will be eager to read about**. It'll be related to your industry and be of urgent interest to your prospects.

3. *I don't have time to write a book* – **Who does?** If you're like me and you're in business, there barely seems to be enough hours in the day to do all the things you're doing now and still have some time at the end of the day to wind down with your loved ones. Believe me, this won't change – I'm going to show you **how to get your book done** without you having to glue yourself to that computer screen for hours every day.

4. *I don't know how to get a book deal with a publisher* – I have great news for you – **you never have to contact a single 'regular' publishing company** – I'll take you through the process of creating books which look like they belong on a bookstore shelf – without working with a regular publisher at all.

5. *I don't have professional printing equipment* – This is part of the deal – **you don't need to print a thing!** You'll discover how get your books printed for you, at a fraction of the cost you are probably dreading right now – **it really is dirt cheap, less than a cup of coffee.**

Now, we're going to talk about publishing your book – but when we talk about it, you and me, we're just talking about getting it into the 'form' of a book – for the purpose of The Ultimate Business Card, we don't care if it *never* appears on a bookstore's shelves.

"Far and away the best prize that life offers is the chance to work hard at work worth doing."
—Theodore Roosevelt

There are 2 ways you can publish your book:

1. **Get a 'book deal'.** This is **not** going to be our preferred option. For a start, it can be very difficult to get a book deal, even if all you want to be is a writer. It doesn't matter how well you write, it doesn't matter how relevant and current your information is, it doesn't matter how urgent the need of your market to get this information, or how eager they are to buy your book as soon as is humanly possible...it is statistically unlikely, you will ever get a book deal. End of story.

   This is because **all unsolicited manuscripts,** when sent to a publisher, go into what they refer to in the industry as a 'slush pile'. To be honest, whenever I hear the term 'slush pile', I can't help but imagine a modestly sized office in the city, with creamy/brown-ish carpet and a huge unkempt pile of A4 size manuscripts loosely piled up in the middle of the room. No matter how well you present your work to the publisher, this is where it ends up.

Every so often, a relatively lowly paid employee will be tasked with the job of going through this slush pile, to see if there's anything worthy of further consideration. I don't envy those who seek to make a living as a writer, having to rely on this grossly inefficient system to get published. What if this lowly paid employee is having an off day? Before the information age, before the technology we have now, if you wanted something that looked and felt like a book, this was the only path open to you. Luckily for us, **we need never submit our book to any publishing company**. Never.

Then, if you somehow, miraculously, wade your way through the masses of the slush pile, end up in an editor's hands and connect with their needs sufficiently that you actually get published, that doesn't mean anything. The publisher will send boxes and boxes of books to your home or office, because they get a better printing rate that way. You're paying for the printing out of whatever money they do pay you. And the unsold books go on your tab, many authors actually end up owing the publisher money. Now, you may receive help with design and formatting, but I'm going to show you that you don't need it – and I'll show you how to order as many or as few books as you want – even just one – without paying anywhere near a retail book price.

2. **Self-publish!** Now **YOU** can become your own publisher...and **YOU are in control**. No need to rely on some overworked, underpaid staff member sifting through their slush pile and surfacing with **YOUR** book over all the others – <u>you don't need them!</u>

I'm about to take you through the entire process of self-publishing – from start to finish. So if you've ever wanted to become a real published author – but didn't know how to get started – this is you lucky day…this is your chance.

Do you really _need_ a book?

Here's the thing – I can't help you get famous – but I can help you get rich…

These are the things we are **NOT** going do:

- **We are NOT** going to try and get you on TV, on the radio, our aim is not to get your face plastered all over the place (Although if you decide you want this, your new book will be an invaluable tool)
- **We are NOT** looking to get your book onto bookstore shelves – this would be a good bonus, but it's harder than you think. Bookstores buy their books from a list sent to them by an agency – and they're mostly looking for established authors, especially now that the internet has caused the closure of so many bookstores – they want books from authors they **KNOW** people will be looking for – they just can't afford to risk shelf space to a book they aren't sure about
- **We are NOT** trying to get you booked on a whirlwind speaking tour, doing presentations every day and selling books from the back of the room (Again – if this is something you want to go after later on – your book will open doors here as well)
- **We are NOT** going to set up a website and spend thousands of dollars in advertising to sell your book – I have a **much more interesting and profitable way** to get your books into the hands of your prospects – and you're going to find it's vastly cheaper than forking out thousands of dollars on newspaper and magazine ads, then making a small handful of sales.

Please understand: having a book on your resume, being a published author, definitely opens plenty of doors. It's a secret weapon which gives you an unfair advantage over every other business in your industry. It's a great positioning tool within your local market – how many of your competitors have their own published books? It's possible someone might have one.

However...are they using the book correctly? Are they using it the way we're going to talk about here, or are they just trying to get on TV and/or trying to make money by selling the book?

You are not going to focus on selling your book. Sure, you will make sales, but mere book sales are not going to be able to compete with the business model I'm about to show you.

We are going to focus on giving your book away. It's the **Ultimate Business Card.**

"Go APE: Author a great book, Publish it quickly and Entrepreneur your way to success. Self-publishing isn't easy, but it's fun and sometimes even lucrative. Plus, your book could change the world."
>   *—Guy Kawasaki, APE: Author, Publisher,*
>   *Entrepreneur. How to Publish a Book*

"Even if you are on the right track, you'll get run over if you just sit there."
>   *— Will Rogers*

Get this:
- **Your book instantly gives you <u>authority</u> and <u>credibility</u>** in your local market. It's all based on people's perceptions. Basically, if someone has written a book on a subject, that automatically makes them an expert on that subject, in the eyes of most people. It doesn't matter that you are already an expert – it doesn't matter that you have been in business for X number of years, have many satisfied customers, if you are a published author, then **there is no question**, you become the go-to person in your industry.

And even a self-published book does this – I'm going to help you make your book look like, feel like, smell like a bookstore book – most people will never realise it wasn't a big agency that published your book

- **Your book won't be thrown out** – let's face it – how many business cards have you kept over the years? Even if they don't get dropped into the bin straight away, there's always that drawer at home, or in the office, where all the business cards go, piled up and shut away until they finally do get removed.

  Even if you keep them all, even if you file them away, scan them into the computer, keeping all the relevant contact details – what are the chances of those cards ever being used? Your book will go on a shelf and will become a resource to be pulled out later on, referred to by someone with a problem to solve – and **your book is there to offer them a solution** – which will of course be to contact you.

- **Your book can be re-used** – if the person you give it to decides they don't want it for whatever reason, it *still* won't be thrown out – it'll be passed on to someone else. Whether it's donated to the local charity shop, or given to a friend, or sold for $1 at a garage sale – it will now move into the hands of a fresh new prospect, who may have never met you or heard of your business – but now **you are 'there' with this new prospect**, with authority, when they need an answer to a problem your business solves.

- **Your book creates what I refer to as 'reciprocity'** – if someone gives you a gift you feel is valuable, don't you feel obligated to give them something in return? I'm not talking about *guilt* at all – people only feel *guilty* when they've done something wrong. Basically, when you give someone your book, that little voice in their head tells them they need to make it up to you – and what better way than to buy from your business? You don't need to 'sell' them on this at all – just tell them to read the book and they'll find your offer in there. You won't believe the number of **people doing business with you as a direct result of your gift**.

- **Your book gets remembered** – the 'corporate handshake', the handing out of small pieces of paper with phone numbers on them, is so overdone, so commonplace and clichéd, it's easily swept under the rug in our minds and quickly forgotten.

Every time I give someone a book, (my secret weapon) I see the look of surprise, even shock, on their face – most of the time they're expecting me to hand them a business card but then a big smile comes over their face and beaming ear to ear, the cursory 'thanks' they were preparing to give me, turns into a warm, heartfelt expression of genuine gratitude which makes me glad I gave it to them. Aside from the obvious business benefits we're getting into here, personally, **it feels great** to provide a hard working entrepreneur with valuable information they can take and implement in their business and at no cost to them.

- **Your book is a much better advertising media than a business card** – in fact, most business cards I see don't actually do any advertising at all. Simply having your name and number on the card, doesn't give anyone a reason to call and buy something. There are ways around this, but a scrap of paper doesn't give you much room to advertise.

However, something you can do freely in your book is advertise your products and services – there's **no problem at all** in mentioning your offers at the start, end and even throughout your book, as long as it doesn't take away from the content. If you do it properly, your readers won't mind – in fact when they become interested in doing business with somebody...you'll be right there with your ad. The content is important of course, but there's nothing wrong with a brief sales pitch either.

- **Your book can generate new business for you for years, even <u>decades</u>** – I've got an old copy of a book called **"Stay Alive All Your Life"** by Norman Vincent Peale, a motivational speaker, it's a good book, I refer to it now and then and I've had it for a while. The thing is...it was printed in 1957. As I'm writing this...it has been on different shelves for the last fifty-seven years. That's nearly six decades his message has been brought into various homes and offices – it's a bit tattered around the edges, the paper slightly yellowed, but otherwise it's still going strong.

Imagine YOUR book still being read by your target market...decades after it was printed... imagine the sheer numbers of the enquiries and sales it would have generated by then – look, Mr. Peale's book doesn't really have much promotion in it, other than a list of his other books at the end, they simply didn't know what we know today – in 57 years when **YOUR** book is still being read by people in your target market – it could still be as powerful a marketing machine as it will be the day it's first sold.

"At heart, self-publishing is kind of like a bake sale. The end product does not need to resemble the one that comes from a commercial bakery, but it must taste good. No-one wants the lumpy under- baked oatmeal cookies with spinach and alfalfa flavoured chips."

—D. C. Williams

"Traditional publishers aim to publish hundreds of thousands of copies of a few books, self-publishing companies make money by publishing 100 copies of hundreds of thousands of books."

— David Carnoy

"The free charts on Amazon are constantly trawled by people with voracious reading appetites. Getting read is an obvious way to sell more copies via word of mouth."

—Ben Galley

"The best self-promotion is your next book. And the book after that and after that..."

—Bella Andre

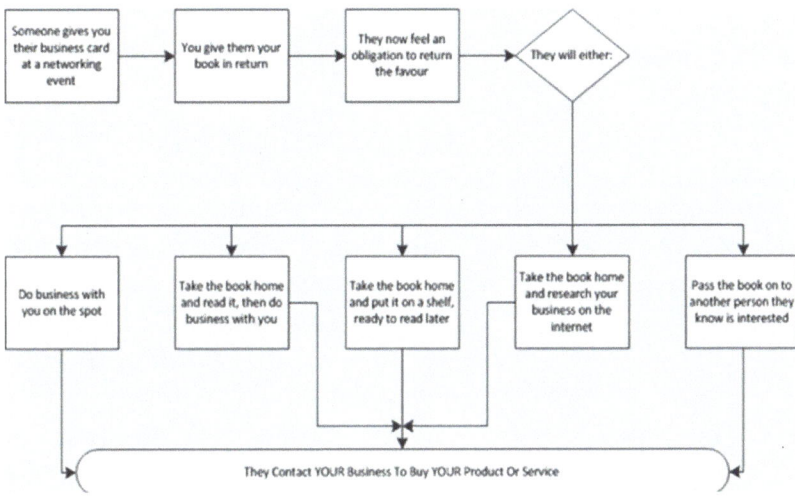

Here's how it works in a nutshell:

Simple as that! Once you have a well- written book, it'll keep bringing in new customers, prospects, clients and patients for as long as you care to stay in business. It's a tireless tool which never sleeps. It's your silent salesman who never asks for time off.

It'll even get people talking about your book on social media like Facebook, **as you can see on the right.**

Facebook and Twitter are also going to be great places you can meet people to send your book to. It's not like buying a mailing list or running an ad – once you start up a conversation with someone on Facebook, then offer to send them your book, this is almost as good as handing them one at an event. Social media is a place to build relationships – and nothing kicks off a good relationship quite like a book. It's the ultimate business card.

"Chase the vision, not the money, the money will end up following you."
—Tony Hsieh, Zappos CEO

"Your work is going to fill a large part of your life, and the only way to be truly satisfied is to do what you believe is great work. And the only way to do great work is to love what you do."
—Steve Jobs, Apple Inc. co-founder,
Chairman and CEO

"Don't worry about failure; you only have to be right once."
—Drew Houston, Dropbox

"Fail often so you can succeed sooner."
—Tom Kelley, Ideo partner

"Whatever you may have heard, self-publishing is not a short cut to anything. Except maybe insanity. Self-publishing, like every other kind of publishing, is hard work. You don't wake up one morning good at it. You have to work for that."
—Zoe Winters, Smart Self-Publishing:
Becoming an Indie Author

CASE STUDY #1: SIMON TUPMAN – SOLICITOR

Book Title: Why Lawyers Should Eat Bananas
Pages: 144

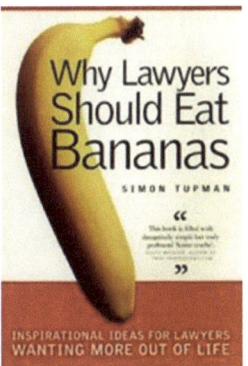

Industry: Lawyers and solicitors

Simon is the director of 'Simon Tupman Presentations,' the organisation he founded in 1994 to provide professional practices with the business knowledge and motivation to counter the challenges of change and competition. Since then the organisation has built up an extensive client base across a range of industries, notably the legal profession.

Simon started life as a solicitor in England in the mid-1980s. His presentations are renowned for practical, relevant and inspiring information.

If you search on Amazon for Simon's book, there are some second hand copies available – but no new books. This shows you his strategy – he has control over the book – he doesn't want to hand someone a book at an event…and have them say *"Oh I bought it on Amazon last week"*. The book is also a great quality publication – Simon offers inspiration ideas for lawyers who want to improve their life just as much as they do their practice. It's a major credibility booster for him and well over a decade after it was first published…it's still going strong.

It's Simon's **Ultimate Business Card**.

Case Study #2: Brett McFall – Online Marketing

Book Title: How To Make Money While You Sleep
Pages: 224

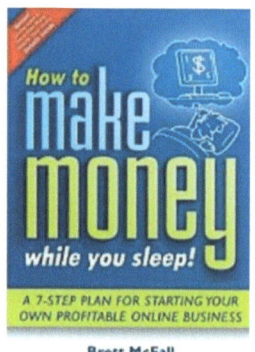

Industry: Internet Marketing Coaching

Brett is best known for teaching people how to make money on the internet quickly and easily. Brett is an international speaker, copywriter and internet marketer. His websites turn over in excess of $500,00 per year practically on autopilot, allowing him to take a holiday somewhere in the world every eight weeks and live the life of his dreams.

Brett is a failed English student from the western suburbs of Sydney but today Brett is regarded by many as Australia's best direct-response copywriter. And he is one of the co-creators of The World Internet Summit, the largest internet business event in the world, teaching thousands of people in Australia, the US, the UK and Asia how to make money online.

One of the ways Brett attained his stunning success is using this book as <u>a lead generation tool</u>. Throughout the book you'll find excellent information, as well as plenty of advertising for Brett's other products and services. This way, he's built up an email list of thousands of people.

Brett sells his book online, in bookstores and at his seminars, to 'cast the net' as wide as he can and build up as large a loyal following as he can. And who can argue with his success. He's a master of multiple marketing methods, including his **Ultimate Business Card**.

26

CASE STUDY #3: JENNY CARTWRIGHT – SALES TRAINER

Book Title: Don't Get Hung Up!
Pages: 157+

Industry: Sales Training

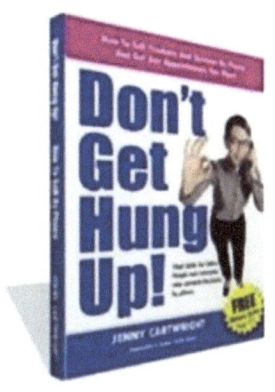

In the 1990's Jenny Cartwright was a prominent and well-respected telemarketing expert. From 1991-997 through direct mail and telemarketing campaigns, Jenny successfully promoted Tom Hopkins, Anthony Robbins, Zig Ziglar, James Rohn, Brian Tracy, Dennis Waitley, Harvey McKay, Michael Gerber and Jay Abraham. Since 1995 Jenny has been accredited as a Trainer and has conducted in-house customer sales, telesales and customer service training for companies and individuals around Australia.

Jenny keeps her book under such a degree of control; **she only sells it on her website**, or **hands it out to prospects**. Jenny also has a few other books available there, as well as some higher priced services.

Whenever she hands out a book, or sells one online, her buyer reads the book and in their mind, Jenny becomes the foremost authority on sales training in Australia.

Jenny's book 'Don't Get Hung Up!' gives people vital skills for conducting business on the phone. Her ultimate business card is an excellent selling tool for her and shows people how to sell products and services by phone and get any appointments you want.

CASE STUDY #4: MICHELLE BOWDEN – PRESENTATION COACH

Book Title: Don't Picture Me naked
Pages: 307

Industry: Presentation Skills

As a speaker who has delivered over 50 presentations and keynotes I still find I need all the help I can get. When I met Michelle Bowden at an event a few years ago I was struck by her professionalism and could not wait to get my hands on her book.

She has chosen a great title for her book – it attracts attention and it ties in with her subject matter...regarding the age-old advice to picture an audience naked, if you are nervous when speaking in public.

In addition, her title suggests that she does not agree with this advice and has a few different ideas on how to speak well in front of people.

Her book shows us once and for all that anyone can be 'an influential presenter' who speaks with confidence, clarity and influence. It is her ultimate business card that reinforces her credibility in the marketplace and she happily signs these wherever she goes with a beautiful engaging smile.

Combined with the power of her ultimate business card, it's no wonder she is so successful.

CASE STUDY #5: JUSTIN HERALD – SUCCESS COACH

Book Title: It's All A Matter Of Attitude
Pages: 110

Industry: Success Coaching

The true essence of what I am sharing with you can be succinctly summed up in the title of this book written by **Justin Herald**. If you want to change someone's life a book can and will do it ... if it is executed properly and with your own personal branding. Imagine having a lasting and profound influence on your reading public who respect and admire you.

Such is the case of Justin Herald who made a strong impression on me when I was going through a difficult period in the early 2000's. At that time, I had returned to teaching and was feeling *frustrated with my life*. By chance I saw an impressive picture on a billboard on the Gold Coast highway in 2001, there was Justin's picture staring at me straight in the face. Never being one to think too long and hard about buying a book, I immediately purchased this 'straight-shooter's' wisdom. It instantly uplifted me. This is a great example of the ultimate business card. My students related to his words of wisdom and wrote them on their folders, "Go Hard or Go Home" was one of their favourites.

Justin's tagline is 'slogans to live by' and he is renowned for taking **Attitude Inc** – the company he founded with only $50, to international success. He is currently regarded as one of the rising stars in the fields of life improvement and personal development. He was once selected as "International Entrepreneur of the Year' which is an impressive accolade and his ultimate business card, 'It's All a Matter of Attitude' helped him get there. When is going to be **YOUR** turn?

When are YOU going to get YOUR 21st Century Business Card?

CASE STUDY #6: NEIL WATERHOUSE – EBAY

Book Title: Million Dollar eBay Business From
Home
Pages: 110

Industry: Online Auctions

Late last year when I was running Networking Events with up to 50 people I was approached by Neil Waterhouse, a Million Dollar eBay Seller. He had heard about my events and a mutual friend introduced us. We chatted for a while and after agreeing to engage him as a speaker at my next business event, Neil immediately asked for my address.

"Why do you need my address?" I asked him. "Nikki, I have a book I wish to send you." Neil insisted that sending his book was the best option, so I could receive it on my doorstep. He reminded me that prospects and clients appreciated receiving a book in the post. When the book arrived, I immediately read it and completed it in 2 days. The power of the ultimate business card never fails when it is sent by Australia Post. Think of Australia Post as doing your marketing for you.

This was the dealmaker for me. If you send your 21st Century Business Card to your prospect, you will leave an even better impression. I was so impressed with Neil that I have happily recommended him to my colleagues and it is clear that his success is due to his knowledge and expertise which shines through in his book.

Neil was using his ultimate business card before I even met him.

CASE STUDY #7: DR MARCIA BECHEREL & DR OLIVIER BECHEREL – ANXIETY

Book Title: Farewell To Anxiety- 7 Quick And Easy Steps
To Rid Yourself Of Anxiety!
Pages: 140

Farewell to Anxiety
7 Quick & Simple Steps to rid yourself of anxiety

Dr Marcia Becherel
Dr Olivier J. Becherel

Industry: Anxiety Treatments

As you have already guessed I do attend many Seminars and this is where I meet most of my clients and get 90% of my business.

At a recent event a few years ago, which went for several days I met an interesting couple, who were using the ultimate business card principle very effectively. Many people would not ordinarily imagine doctors creating a book, let alone using it as a marketing tool, but it has worked out for them very well and here's why...

Their book showcases their knowledge and gives a lot of information away for free! This immediately dispels the myth that doctors always charge high prices. If they are giving away important information then they must be good! These doctors are no general practitioners. They are both Master Practitioners of NLP, Time Line Therapy and Hypnosis. They provide life and wellness coaching on a 'holistic approach to self-empowerment by integrating their wealth of knowledge to quickly achieve optimum health.' Their message is powerful and on the back of their book it reads...

"DON'T READ THIS BOOK! Unless you are ready to get rid of panic attacks, pounding heart and cold chills".

If you suffer from Anxiety then being handed this book is not only going to help you with your symptoms – it will also create the perception (quite fairly in this case) that these authors are the foremost experts in their field.

"Twenty years from now you will be more disappointed by the things that you didn't do than by the ones you did do. So throw off the bowlines. Sail away from the safe harbour. Catch the trade winds in your sails. Explore. Dream... Discover."

—Mark Twain, Author

CASE STUDY #8: MICHELE GILLETT & SHARRON – DEL WAKELY – CONSULTANTS

Book Title: Classy And Fabulous
Pages: 83

Industry: Fashion Consulting

If you are an image consultant, stylist then the ultimate business card is complimentary to your business and absolutely essential. Michele and Sharron-Del are the founders of "Absolutely Fabulous Colour And Style" an image consultancy that assists people to realise their true visual potential.

They love working with the power of line, design and colour to transform the way people dress, accessorise and shop. "We have so much fun working together and we want to pass on the excitement and passion we have what we do, to our clients," Michele says.

And what better way to pass that energy along than via a well written book? It's only 83 pages long – a prime example of quality over quantity.

Their ultimate business card has branded them as the ultimate guide to stylish dressing.

CASE STUDY #9: ROBYN HENDERSON – NETWORKER

Book Title: What My Favourite Teacher Taught Me
Pages: 185

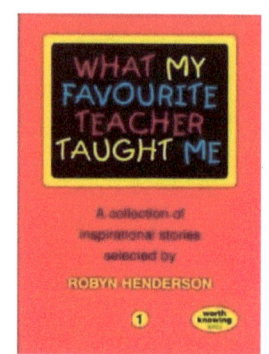

Industry: Networking

No person on this planet or in this city is more symbolic of the ultimate business card than the lady herself, Robyn Henderson. Robyn has written many books all of which touch on her various experiences particularly in the area of Networking. This book however resonates with me and was given to me as a prize at a SWAP Networking Event in Sydney in 2012. I treasure this book because of the stories contained within it and Robyn's reference to sunrise...

She writes, *"If you have never seen a sunrise, plan to see one within the next month. I hope you see a 15/10 sunrise that it will take your breath away. Your heart will fill with love and emotion just to be in the presence of such beauty. Mother Nature is beautiful, consistent, reliable, sturdy, yet at the same time so fragile. Mother Nature is my teacher."*

These are fitting words of proof that your 21st Century Business Card is indeed your ticket to riches, fame, success, recognition, abundance and prosperity.

Robyn has also published a second volume of the book, as pictured on the left, with more inspirational stories, more fantastic information and more credibility in the eyes of her prospects.

CASE STUDY #10: MATT CHURCH, PETER COOK AND SCOTT STEIN – SOCIAL MEDIA

Book Title: Sell Your Thoughts
Pages: 252

__Industry: Social Media Marketing__

You would be well aware of the power of social media. Well, here's a powerful example of this in action. Right now, I have a green covered book, which was sent to me by a contact on LinkedIn who reached out to me and offered to send me a book for FREE. This contact immediately sent the book, within a day and I received it with a follow-up phone call. I am now hoping to do business with this contact. Why? Because first impressions are the strongest. If Peter Cook has the energy and enthusiasm to contact me on LinkedIn and follow-up, then I want to learn more, know more and gain more from this relationship.

This book has a magnificent tagline, "**How to Earn a Million Dollars a Year as a Thought Leader.**" The blurb on the back is equally compelling. This book is a 'call to action', an invitation for you to bring your thinking into the world. This book is about moving from someone who knows something to someone who is known for knowing something and able to derive fabulous commercial gain.

The benefits on the back cover state "the concepts, insights and strategies laid out in this book are invaluable for an expert looking to have a greater impact with their ideas."

This gets the reader interested in the contents – and if your prospect is interested and reads your book, then acts on its advice, they are much more likely to do business with you in the future.

This is the power of the ultimate business card.

CASE STUDY #11: BRIAN CASSINGENA – COPYWRITER

Book Title: Copywriting Secrets Of Million Dollar Marketers Revealed
Pages: 251

Industry: Advertising & Marketing

Brian recently sent me his book on advertising and copywriting – and suddenly I was introduced into a whole new world of online and offline marketing – because in the book he interviews a number of the best marketing and copywriting experts from all over the world. This is the ultimate business card because:

- It associates Brian's name with the well-known marketers being interviewed.
- He has included some testimonials from clients in the book to show he gets results.
- He has promotions throughout the book for his prospects to do business with him.
- He has even set up a member's area for readers of the book where you can listen to the interviews and download a number of marketing resources

So this begs the next question...

HOW DO YOU WRITE A BOOK?

It's a fair question – and by the end of this book you are going to feel very excited about getting your own book in paper-and-ink. By now you're probably thinking: "How on earth am I going to find time to write a book?" You've probably heard stories of authors sitting at the computers (or typewriters), typing away for hours and hours every day and night, weekends as well, churning out their innermost thoughts to create their book.

I'm going to show you some of the ways we create books – we'll start at the least efficient and work our way up to the most efficient way to get yourself published.

Method 1: *Sit down and write your book* – now, for the purposes of your 21st Century Business Card, I am going to advise against this age-old, standard approach of manual labour, working long hours, pumping out your blood sweat and tears to create a pristine, perfect manuscript which will be toasted as the ultimate text in its industry.

We don't want to do this. If you are determined to write a best-selling masterpiece then that's genuinely wonderful – but at least wait until we finish your 21st Century Business Card before you do so. Your business is ready & waiting for new customers – let's start feeding it now.

You don't need a thoroughly thought out and immaculately written book. You don't need perfection.

You don't need a 'War And Peace'– you just need something that will <u>work</u>.

And what will work best for you is a simple, easy-to-read book written in plain English that everyone can understand, which can be created in a very short period of time.

Remember – your customers may not be as educated as you and they probably don't know the technical terms used in your business. Whenever I take my car to the mechanic, I don't want to know about the pistons or the fuel pump or the spark plugs, or how the work together – as long as the mechanic makes my car work. It's the benefit I want – the benefit of having a car that gets me from A to B, I don't need to know the inner workings of the engine to drive the car successfully.

So don't fill up your book with technical terms the average person may not be aware of – if you confuse them, they'll put down your book and you've lost them.

The other problem here is speed – or *lack of it*. I know *people* – and no matter how excited they are now about doing something, even if it's close to their hearts, even if they know in their heads that it'll reap huge benefits, such as writing this kind of book, I know that if the process starts to drag on too long, if it gets drawn out unnecessarily, if it becomes too much work, then life gets in the way, things come up and projects get put on the back burner.

This is a danger you must avoid. If you simply must craft your book carefully with your own hand, be sure and do it quickly, strike while the iron is hot. Or you risk looking back in a year and finding a half-finished book and realising it could have been bringing in new business over that whole year.

This brings me to my next point – keep it brief! If you can write with lightning speed – great – but the benefits are mostly nullified if you decide to write another 'War And Peace.' That enormous, 1,225 page book took years to write – you don't have years, your customers will have gone elsewhere by then.

And don't fall for the trap of overfilling it with too much content just for the sake of bulk. In this day and age, where everyone seems to have the attention span of a computer-addicted teenager on a constant diet of energy drinks, people find thick books much less appealing. They just take time to read. And we all seem to be short of time these days, right?

Are you going to dedicate all your spare time to writing a book? Are you going to come home from the shop or office, have a quick bite to eat, then park yourself in front of the computer all night, for the next few months or even years? Personally I'd rather spend time with my loved ones, family and friends, so fortunately <u>there are alternatives</u>…

Method 2: Have your book written for you! This is the subject of some confusion, people either seem to think it's cheating, or a way to get a crappy book written, or just plain wrong. I'm going to demonstrate to you how this method gets you a great book, while allowing you to sleep at night knowing you've done no wrong.

They're called "**Ghostwriters**" – people who write books, manuals and other content for other people, in return for a fee. And they're a whole lot more common than you probably realise…

- **The Diary Of Anne Frank (Actually written by her father)**
- **H.P. Lovecraft wrote a book for Harry Houdini**
- **Tom Clancy's Splinter Cell book series is written by various ghostwriters**
- **To Kill A Mockingbird**
- **I am Jackie Chan, by Jackie Chan and Jeff Yang (but probably just Jeff Yang)**

And plenty more. A lot of commercial music is not written by the artist who sings on the album. Mozart even ghostwrote music for other composers before achieving fame with his own music.

Many celebrities and politicians use ghostwriters, whenever you see a book authored by that celebrity and the additional line "With (insert unknown author here)" as equal writing credits on the front cover – it's unlikely the celebrity in question did much actual writing.

And **entrepreneurs love Ghostwriters**. Stephen Covey, Jack Welch, Richard Branson, Sam Walton of Walmart, Donald Trump, they all used ghostwriters for at least part of the writing work. However, there's something I need you to understand…

There is nothing wrong with using a ghostwriter

It happens all the time – and some of our most loved books, movies and music are created by one person, then credited to another. Ghostwriters perform a valuable service in bringing quality information to people, in the form of a book or a movie and they waive their right to the spotlight in exchange for a fee. Most of them do not seek out fame anyway, so it's a win-win situation. This is from **Lou Gerstner, the former CEO of IBM**, from his book "Who Said Elephants Can't Dance?"…

"I wrote this book without the aid of a co-author or a ghostwriter (which is why it's a good bet this is going to be my last book)I had no idea it would be so hard"

There are plenty of places you can get your book ghostwritten. One I have used is http://eLance.com or http://oDesk.com. These are online communities where you can post a project, then people bid on it and all you do is choose the winning bidder and they complete your project.

According to the Journal of the European Medical Writers Association, 42% of academic medical papers are ghostwritten

One word of warning: Many of the workers who will bid on your projects are from countries like Bangladesh, Pakistan, India and eastern European countries. And while they're lovely people and often do fantastic technical work like web design, computer programming and graphic design and at prices you won't believe;

their English spelling and grammar skills are often not up to par.

This means if you get something ghostwritten, the delivered book won't be ready to go – you'll need to post another project to have it cleaned up, edited, formatted, you could end up going through a few different contractors trying to get a decent book written.

There *are* plenty of workers from English speaking countries – but they will tend to charge much more for their services. However, often their delivered product won't need any editing at all.

Here's how you can get your book ghostwritten without fuss or lengthy delays.

Step 1. Choose your angle. This is your overall theme for your book – and it'll depend largely on what business you are in. And it's important to get this figured out early on and written down on paper, before you start paying to get stuff done. Otherwise you'll end up having something written, then if you change your mind or your strategy later, you'll have perfectly good material you can't use. And the time taken will also be wasted.

The angle you take can also be used in the book title. Here are some ideas for common businesses:

- Chiropractor – **3 Ways To A Pain Free Body** – Here you can include some tips on posture, chair & mattress selection and other techniques to keep the spine aligned. You can have plenty of ads for your practice in the book and you could mail it to a list of prospects, as a way to get them in for a 1st appointment.
- Accountant – **How To Double Your Tax Return** – Include some simple ideas people can use to claim deductions on their tax return and in all likelihood they'll just end up having you do their return anyway. Or, you could specialise in businesses and provide information for business owners on minimising corporate taxes. And of course, throughout the book you can explain the ways you do this for clients.

- Computer Repair – **Free PC Self-Check Procedure** – Describe, in layman's terms of course, a few easy ways that even non-technical people can ensure their PC is running as well as it should be. One great bonus you could add is a CD-ROM – or even create a download area on your website, where they can download software.
- Mechanic – **7 Ways To Keep Your Car Purring Like A Kitten** – Show some of the common problems you encounter with customers' cars and how they can be easily avoided with a few minutes of preventative maintenance. If you're the expert mechanic in town, people who want the best quality maintenance for their car will see you as the obvious choice.
- Health Food Store – **Food Additive Numbers Decoded** – Explain about all the harmful food additives that are in the food people eat every day, which ones to avoid, which ones trigger certain disorders and so on. Then you can present some natural substitutes and if you have an online store of some kind, it's very easy to include links to purchase these alternatives.

I could list a dozen more ideas for a dozen more businesses – whatever common problem your customers, clients or patients come to you with – that's what you can write the book about. That's your angle. The actual information is less important than the positioning of expert and the free gift you're giving. This is not to say the contents of the book don't matter, they do – it still has to be reasonably good. But if you want to write the definitive text on your subject and write the greatest book in your industry, then please do, but that'll take too long for our purposes here.

Step 2. Get the book written. There are many ways to do this. One way is to write it yourself. If you must do this – get cracking – before someone else in your industry beats you to it. If you're fine with hours on the computer and you write very quickly, then please do so.

If you want to get your 21st Century Business Card working for you as soon as possible and you can see how your customers are ready and waiting for someone to announce themselves as the local expert, then there are many sources of books, such as eLance.com, oDesk.com, FreeLancer.com and others.

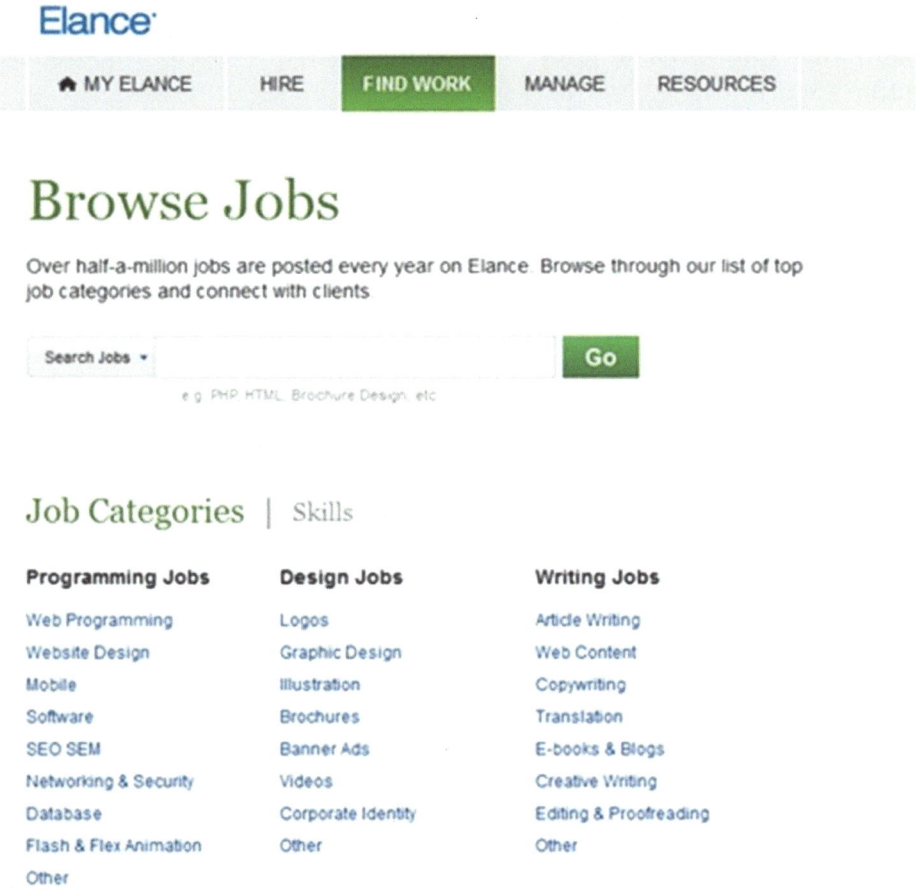

eLance.com is one of the most popular online websites for outsourcing work. As of this writing, there have been 113,866 projects posted in the last 30 days for workers to complete, ranging from book writing to computer programming, data entry, even financial planning and taxation services. And there are 3,447,682 registered workers waiting for you to post your job. It's a big site.

You can post a job and hire someone either by the hour, or for a fixed amount. Make sure you describe what you want clearly and choose a budget for your project. Once it's posted, bids will start to come in. You'll be able to sort them by price, although this is often a false economy – remember, the lowest bids might sound appealing, but anything written by them will probably have to be edited and formatted properly. You can choose workers from English speaking countries and their higher fees will often be worth the higher quality work.

There is no charge to post a project. eLance takes a 8.75% cut of the worker's payment for each project, so they pay, not you. They can also buy a monthly membership to be able to connect with more employers.

Make sure you inspect all the work samples they'll send and read the proposals. Once you hire someone, you'll need to pay the money to eLance, they'll keep it in escrow until you approve the finished work sent to you.

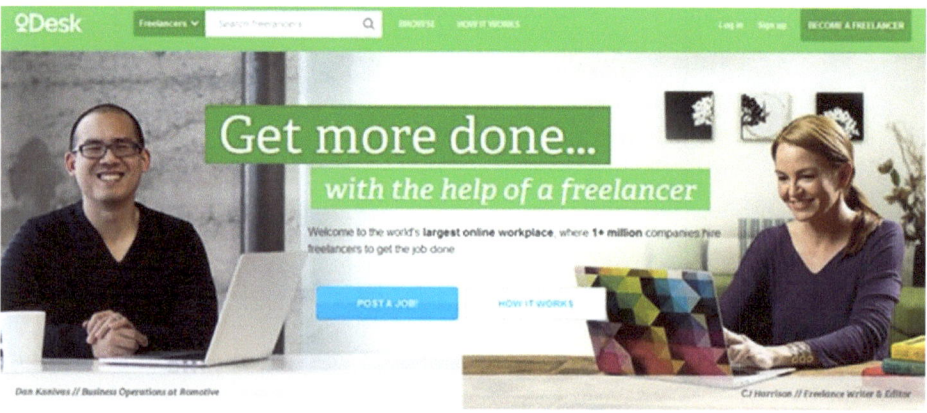

www.upwork.com is a handy site for getting work done for an hourly rate. This is more like a typical employee situation, except for the fact that they're probably on the other side of the world and you generally only need pay a fraction of a western minimum wage.

However if the project goes over time, it'll also go over budget and a good worker might be worth it, but it's sometimes hard to pick a good one. You can see the portfolio of a worker and they can earn a shield which allows you to get a refund, if you're not happy with the work within a certain timeframe.

www.upwork.com has a 'team room' feature which allows you to view the activity levels of your worker – this means their level of keyboard and mouse activity. And, you can get web cam and screenshot images of them working.

www.upwork.com charges a 10% fee of whatever you pay the worker, in the same way that eLance works.

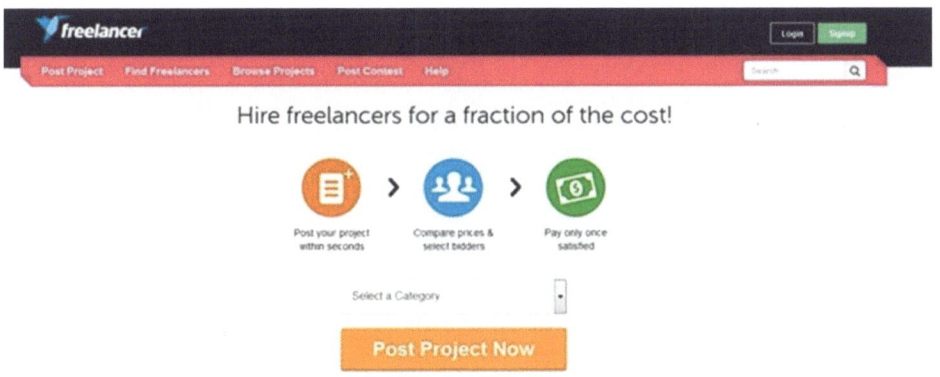

FreeLancer.com is another online marketplace where you can find workers. Their fee structure is a bit more complicated, they charge a 3% fee for fixed projects or 10% for hourly projects, unless you're on one of their 2 highest priced plans, which are $50 and $200 a month. The fee structure seems confusing so take a look around the site before you post a job.

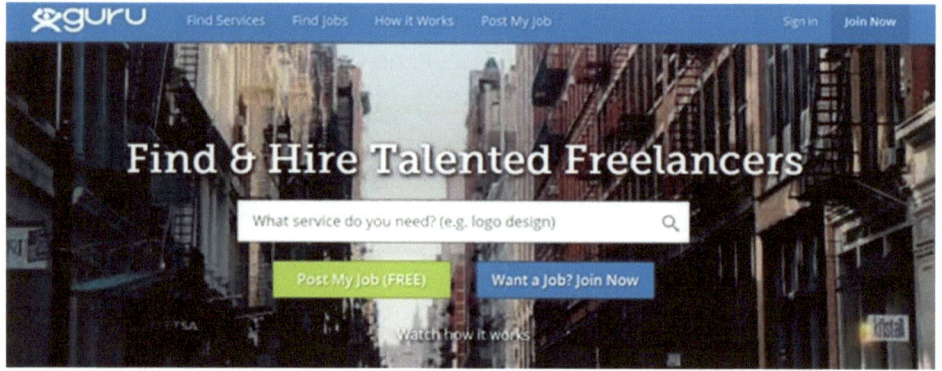

<u>Guru.com</u> charges a 2.45% free to post a project if you pay by credit card or PayPal and they deduct a percentage of the worker's payment, depending on their membership level. However if you build up money in a Guru.com account, such as for doing work, or from a deposit, they don't charge the 2.45% fee for that. Alternately you can send a cheque, or use a US bank account to avoid the fee.

It's quite simple to get your book written. I'll outline the procedure here, however, all projects are different in various ways and you'll be able to manage each one, dealing with the inevitable issues as they come up, which they will. For this example we'll be using eLance, one of the most popular sites.

1. Go to your website of choice, sign up for an account and post your project. Add a credit card as a payment method, on eLance, workers can see when you've added and verified a credit card and **this gives them more incentive** to place a bid.

2. Make sure you post your project in the correct category, for your 21st Century Business Card, you'll want to post it in the *'Writing & Translation'* category and within that, there is a *'Ghostwriting'* category. Most workers are only able to bid for projects in one category of their choosing. You won't get much interest if you post your book writing project in the Database programming category...

3. Give the project a **straightforward title**, something like *"Ghostwrite a (Insert Subject) book"*. Then, clearly describe your project, the length you want the book to be, what kind of subjects you want covered, what you don't want, the key is to be clear and straightforward. Don't use your full vocabulary; many workers will be from non-English speaking backgrounds. Just keep it simple.

4. Read all the proposals which come in. The bidders may attach samples of previous work. Look at these. Look at their proposal; is it a generic template they send to everyone? Or have they sat down and written it just for you?

   Weigh up each proposal. Sort by price, but don't decide purely on price. I promise you are going to get bids of $50 or even less, even if you ask for a 300 page book. Evaluate each one based on whether it's a realistic bid, if you are likely to get a good product, or if you might regret hiring that person.

   Remember that you get what you pay for – if you buy cheap, you get cheap. If you hire someone to write your book for $35, you are going to have to post more projects, just to get that manuscript cleaned up, edited and formatted.

   You need to consider paying as much as you can for the book. The ultimate business card must be something you will be proud to hand out, something you genuinely want people to read, something you hope they pass on to someone else if they're not interested.

5. Take your initial estimate that you thought you were going to spend on a book and double it. At least. Many people on eLance will try to sell you the dream of having a book written for peanuts. It's tempting to hire them, even if you expect to do a lot of editing. However… it's not worth it. Editing takes time and money, whether you are the one who does it or not.

6. If you can afford to go with the highest bidder, or near highest, as long as their native language is English, they are genuine and they have great samples to show you, **hire them**. And be prepared to hire nobody – there is no obligation to award the job to anyone on eLance – because you might not get a bid you feel comfortable with anyway. You might just get unlucky and the good writers, (they do exist), will just miss seeing your job on the site.

7. In reality – expect to pay upwards of $1000 for any half-decent book to be written. You're looking at a 50 page book for that, on your industry, offering advice to people they can use. At these prices you won't have to get the book re-written, edited and so on. It'll be ready to go. If you send the worker the ads you want to put in the book, they can include them, or you can do it later.

8. Once you accept a bid, you'll need to put the funds into escrow. This is where you pay the money to eLance, they look after it and once you approve the final product sent to you, then eLance releases the money to the worker. You can set milestones if you want and release certain amounts once those milestones are achieved by the worker. However, unless you only plan on having 3 chapters in your book, this can become cumbersome.

9. Once the final product is delivered, you will be the full rights owner of it, the worker's name does not need to appear anywhere on it. It will be as if you had written the book yourself. That's the idea!

10. Most writers on eLance do not do book covers, I'm happy to refer you to the designer I use, whose details appear at the start of this book. Or, you can post another project on eLance or one of the other sites.

11. When hiring workers in this way, it's important to prepare yourself. Prepare yourself for frustration, delays, excuses,

copying and pasting, micromanagement, it's all part of **the** fun! Many workers are perfectly competent and will create good work with little fuss, although many of them are the exact opposite. Additionally, they may be in a considerably different time zone to you – but may not realise you're not online at 3am, because that's 11am in their country. Most people understand, but there's always some...

I certainly hope I haven't put you off posting a project to get your book written! Once you get through all that, you should have a quality book which you can use as your 21st Century Business Card. You'll have it usually in word format, which isn't much good to you yet – here's the next step...

HOW TO PUBLISH YOUR BOOK

This is where you get to turn your ordinary word file into a real live paper-and-ink book you can hand out to prospects. The master marketers at Amazon have provided you with a fantastic platform where you can create and publish your book. It's called CreateSpace.

1. Go to http://CreateSpace.com. Register for a free account and log in. You should see a button which says "Add New Title," although as with any website, things may change in the future. However I don't think they will vary greatly from what they are now.

2. After you click the button you'll be able to enter the name of your project, choose the "Paperback" type and choose from either a guided process, with instructions along the way, or an expert process which is just a single page, for those who have done this before. Let's assume this is your first CreateSpace book, so we'll click on Guided.

3. Enter the title information, author (YOU), volume number and book description. If you don't plan to sell the book online at all, this doesn't need to be filled out with any great detail. Click 'Save & Continue'.

4. The next screen allows you to choose the physical properties of your book. Firstly, you can choose from a Black & White or colour interior. Now, unless you really want to invest in making your book look absolutely spectacular, it's probably best to go with black & white for now, as colour printing inside really drives up the cost.

   You can also choose the paper colour, either white or cream and the size of your book. If you're going for that 'bookstore-look' book, 6" by 9" is good. Alternatively, you may want to measure an actual book which you like the size of and see if that size is available.

5. The next screen gives you **ISBN** options. An **ISBN** is the identifying number for all published books. And even if you only ever plan to store books at home and hand them out, you still need one. There are plenty of help pages on **ISBNs** on the CreateSpace page, but for now I would advise you to choose the free **ISBN**, you'll still retain all rights to the book.

6. Once the site has assigned an ISBN to you, it will display a couple of numbers, just like the ones at the beginning of this book. Write these down! You will need to put them on the copyright page of your book before you can publish it. If your book is just waiting for this, then insert the numbers now and create PDF file of your book. Then click Continue.

7. The next stage is to upload the interior files of your book, the actual 'pages'. There are two options, one is to have CreateSpace help you with the formatting, the other is to upload a print ready PDF yourself.

   It's often hard to decide which way to go – unless you are an expert at formatting for CreateSpace, it can be tricky to get your manuscript just right, so that it looks exactly as you want it to look when it's printed. You can see a preview before you order a copy, but many a copy has been ordered, then thrown out because the formatting is all wrong.

   Balance up the cost of professional help, with the benefits of having it down for you. It'll save a lot of time, if you can factor that cost into your marketing budget.

8. Then you'll be able to upload the actual PDF file. For most books you'll want to choose the "Ends Before" Bleed option. This means your content will end before the edge of the page. Click Save & Continue.

9. Once it's uploaded you can create your cover. Of course CreateSpace will be glad to assist you with this as well, or

you can upload a print ready PDF cover, if you have one prepared.

Alternatively, the third choice is to use the 'Cover Creator.' This is a program which helps you to design your cover right on the site, inserting your name, book title and choosing some images and colours. See how you go with this, it can often look very basic on your first attempt and you want it to look its best – make sure you get it right. It's true that we shouldn't judge a book by its cover... but we do.

10. The last step is to confirm everything and submit your files to CreateSpace for review. You have the option of going back and editing any parts of the process you wish, except for the **ISBN** you were given.

Again, there are plenty of help files for you on this page and if all is well, click Submit Files for Review and CreateSpace will check your files and make sure everything is OK.

11. Now you'll be taken to a page where you can enter the full description of your book, if you wish to sell it online. You have a maximum of 4,000 characters to describe your book, so choose your words carefully. You can also choose the language, country of publication, date, keywords and add an Author Biography.

You also need to choose your **category** – then you're ready to set your price!

12. Amazon will show you the minimum price – if you're going to sell it on Amazon as well as using it as your 21st Century Business Card, set the price you want and click 'Save'. Then, Amazon will tell you when you can start ordering books! You'll automatically be charged the minimum price when you're logged in, so order a box and start handing them out!

THE ROAD TO SUCCESS

If you're reading this chapter then **you're in some rare company** – statistically, most people never read all the way to the end of a book, and that's if the book gets read at all, too often you'll find books tucked away on shelves, their spines in mint condition from never being opened, the riches within hidden away perhaps forever.

"It's hard to do a really good job on anything you don't think about in the shower."
> *—Paul Graham, YCombinator co-founder*

"Best startups generally come from somebody needing to scratch an itch."
> *—Michael Arrington, TechCrunch founder*

"Stay self-funded as long as possible."
> *—Garrett Camp, founder of Expa,*
> *Uber and StumbleUpon*

"When I'm old and dying, I plan to look back on my life and say 'wow, that was an adventure,' not 'wow, I sure felt safe.'"
> *—Tom Preston-Werner, Github co-founder*

"I try not to make any decisions that I'm not excited about."
> *—Jake Nickell, Threadless*

However, you've been smart enough to avoid this fate, as you've read through this book you've seen just how powerful a book can be as your 21st Century Business Card. I've shown you:

- **How you can surge ahead of the competition and wow your prospects with a simple, well written book, which doesn't cost you an arm and a leg.**
- Multiple ways to use a book to close twice as many sales as you currently are – while everyone else in your industry wonders how you do it.
- **How to get people seeking YOU out, instead of you chasing new customers all the time – this puts you in a great position to make sales without resistance.**
- The immense authourity and credibility you'll have and the way this instantly makes your prospects want to do business with you, and nobody else.
- **The steps to writing a quality book you'll be proud to have others read – without having to lock yourself away for months, writing.**
- The steps to publishing a book without relying on landing a book deal with a publishing firm, getting trapped in the glut of new books, or filling your garage with boxes of books.
- **11 real life examples of successful Aussie business owners and entrepreneurs using their Ultimate Business Cards to turbo charge their businesses and build their empires**
- How modern technology is finally allowing everyday business owners like you and me to market effectively – even 10 years ago you still would have to get a book deal to do this

And more. You now have the tools you'll need to create and publish a powerful, compelling, effective ultimate business card for yourself. Even with the problems you're faced with.

Problems like getting the book <u>written</u>.
It's an intimidating project for a first time author.

Even if you write the book yourself and there's nothing wrong with that, it could easily turn out to be a 'false economy'. You might save a few dollars on a ghostwriter, but how much are you losing by sitting down for months and piecing a manuscript together?

It's not all about dollars and cents – family life is important too, and with our already full, busy lives, there seems to be less and less of that previous family time. And as a business owner, I know from experience – it's not like we get to 'clock off' at 5pm each day. If you're like me, you're often the last one to leave, by the time you get home, the kids are almost in bed, it's enough to make you wonder where the time has gone.

Perhaps you could spend a few hours late at night, every night, typing it up. I've tried – it makes life prickly with your other half. The other issue is just how creative you are at that time of night – your body is getting ready for sleep and your concentration is going to waver.

So unless you have plenty of free time during the day, or you are a super creative person with tons of fresh ideas bursting forth from your mind every day, we're probably not going to write this thing ourselves.

The next problem is part of what I mentioned earlier – the ghostwriter.

You are statistically unlikely to find the perfect writer for you, on the first project you post online. Most writers on these sites are from countries like India, Pakistan, Bangladesh, and other non-English speaking countries, and God bless them, they're lovely, smart people, but it's difficult to learn not only a new language, but to be fluent enough in that language to write a high quality book which people will enjoy reading.

Sure, you can hire an Australian, UK, US or Canadian writer. However you can expect to pay accordingly – western people in western countries have western sized bills to pay.

So there's the problem of choice – do you accept a low quality manuscript, knowing you'll have to hire other people, perhaps several others, to edit into a publishable state? Or do you pay through the nose to have it written by a western ghostwriter – still with no guarantee it'll be any good – then you've still got a number of problems to deal with:

- **Your book cover** – unless you're a graphic artist, you can't simply create it yourself if you want to look professional – you'll need to pay someone to do it for you. (And don't forget the back cover – it's the second most read part of any book)
- **Editing and formatting** – another job you'll need to pay someone to do, again, this is critical to a quality book...so you'll need it done right
- **Publishing**-This is a big one – it's great to have a top quality book on your computer – especially when you've paid a stack of money and micromanaged a team for months to get it done – but how are you going to get the words on paper without a book deal or a printing company?
- **Hand-holding**...I'm serious about having to micromanage some of these people, often they'll be unable to do much work without sending every page to you for approval, or they'll send several emails per hour, every hour, until you've basically written the entire book yourself after all
- **Time**. It's the same for us all – the passing of time means the passing of opportunities, the chance for a business breakthrough gone begging, because you were stuck working with a ghostwriter. The chance to spend a full evening with your family at home – without having your book constantly intruding into your thoughts, ruining the evening for all of you
- If none of that sounds particularly appealing to you, then you're in the right place at the right time.
- Because I've got the answer for you.

Introducing **Writers Retreats For Budding Entrpreneurs and Authors!....**

How would you like a 100% complete, edited, high quality paperback book? You'll have **your very own** 21st Century business card right there in your hands, ready to go to work for you. I can promise you, there will be:

- **No slaving away** until late every night writing a book, sacrificing your family time or your business's profits, or your sanity.
- **No hiring and firing** ghostwriters, editors, graphic artists, proofreaders, or any of the other extra people you'd normally need to write a book.
- **No waiting** for months and months to get the finished product – you will have it in your hand in 21 days or less – I guarantee it.

There are other book creation programs but you're either paying up to 5 times as much to get in – or you have to wait months and months before you see your book! And those months are going to be tough, it's not easy being in business for yourself…

- **Is your advertising failing to draw the response you need? Is half of your advertising budget wasted, but you don't know which half?**
- Do you wonder how you can get new customers, clients and patients through the door without spending thousands every month, marketing your business?
- **Do you come away from networking meetings with a handful of ordinary business cards, but no real progress? Do the people you give business cards to actually remember you – or do they simply file your card away somewhere to be forgotten?**
- Are you looking for fresh ideas on how to help your prospects understand the true value of your products and services, over your competition?
- **Have you had enough of price matching and slashing your profit margins just to get a customer?**

BENEFITS OF OUR WRITING RETREATS
IN AUSTRALIA AND OVERSEAS

Do you wonder if it is worth your time to attend a writing retreat?

Retreats can act as tremendous confidence builders. Many writers who work alone suffer from "writer's funk" because they get into their own heads and convince themselves that their writing is bad, or even worthless and they should just drop the project.

I will guide you to understand how book writing really happens and help you rekindle your **joy of writing.**

Going on retreat is one of the best methods to fire up your inspiration and enthusiasm.

When the mind encounters new vistas and new surroundings, it begins processing differently, synthesising elements together that you have not thought of before. I call it the The Aha! Factor. The Aha! Factor increases as you finally receive answers to perplexing problems about your writing that you may not have been able to generate without this new environment.

It is often difficult to clear your mind from all your other daily activities and responsibilities so you can focus exclusively on your writing project. Without being able to turn your mind away from all its clutter, most people just cannot be as creative as they need to be when thinking about their book.

In a professionally conducted writing retreat, you can have at your fingertips people who are experts in the ways authoring your book. I have the knowledge and background pertaining to what you need. If you want to publish a non-fiction book, or a fiction book... a retreat is the answer. You have 24/7 access to me and I can help you target your book concept and learn how to write it effectively and efficiently.

You will receive personalised attention throughout the time. Having a few others around can help provide great feedback for your ideas. Other people can act as your own private "focus group" and you can read material to each other and get constructive critiques and a new appreciation for what other people think when they read your work.

My retreats allow time for you to be alone, to reflect, and dig deep into your soul about your project. You need this type of 'deep alone time', away from the hustle and bustle of your regular life, to delve into your thinking and writing. Ideally, the retreat will be structured with some instructional meeting time, one-on-one or in a group, followed by time for you to go it alone for a bit when you can assimilate what you learned and begin testing it out in your writing.

If you are like me, you've had a gutful. I reached that point some years ago – and I took action. It's not easy being in business for yourself – I want to at least make getting new customers easy!

And I'm about to hand you the tools to do just that...

Call me on 0414 638 552 or 02 4471 1564
or skype me lifestyleplus1
or email nikkicooper888@gmail.com

I would love hear from you. I can help you get your book published at one of our fabulous retreats. Let's talk. Take action now. Pick up the phone, shoot me an email, just touch base. I am here to help I have written five books, I have taught English for over 25 years, marked HSC for years I know my stuff. I am your girl. Let's get your book started today! Nothing replaces the excitement of having a book in your hands. your own book.

Speak to you soon and happy writing!

Nikki Cooper